HUNGRY
HUNGRY HEARTS

The miracle of the loaves and fishes,
Matthew 14:13–21; Mark 6:31–44; Luke 9:10–17;
John 6:5–15, for children

Heather Kaufman
Illustrated by Maegan Penley

CONCORDIA PUBLISHING HOUSE · SAINT LOUIS

It was a hot Galilean day,
and Jesus traveled by boat
with His disciples in order to pray
at a place that was far and remote.

But the people all followed Jesus,
for they'd heard of the miracles He'd done.
They cried, "Oh, teach us, Lord, and heal us!
We've heard You're the chosen one!"

Jesus' heart filled with compassion
as He began to heal and teach.
"They're like sheep with no one to lead them,"
He said, blessing all within His reach.

The crowd listened throughout the day,
not realizing how late it'd become,
so intent on what Jesus had to say
that they completely forgot to go home!

Now the crowd was tired and hungry,
with nothing in sight to eat.
The disciples began to get worried.
Feeding this crowd would be quite a feat!

"Where can we find food for so many?"
The disciples all scratched their heads.
"I'm afraid we don't have the money
to buy enough fish or bread."

"And even if we had the money," they cried,
"Where would we go to buy food?"
"We're in the middle of nowhere," they sighed,
"and this crowd's in a munchy mood."

"I have five barley loaves and two fish."
A little boy offered up his lunch.
"But this is too small of a dish
for everyone here to munch."

Jesus smiled at the courageous kid
who'd done what he'd thought right.
"Sit in groups of fifty and one hundred.
We'll be sharing a meal tonight."

Jesus blessed the humble spread
and lifted His voice to God.
"Now give everyone the food," He said.
(His disciples found this quite odd.)

But what's this? One, two, three, four—
the fish and loaves all multiplied!
Five, six, and seven more,
right before the disciples' eyes!

Piece by piece, as the food was broken,
more appeared, endless fish and bread!
It was just as Jesus had spoken—
everyone there would be fed.

So much food and more besides—
twelve baskets filled with broken pieces!
Everyone was full and satisfied
and in awe of the Savior, Jesus.

The little boy grinned ear to ear,
for he'd seen a miracle that day.
God's love and power had appeared
in a most spectacular way.

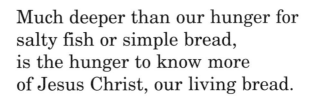

Much deeper than our hunger for
salty fish or simple bread,
is the hunger to know more
of Jesus Christ, our living bread.

Without Him our hearts are empty
and lonely as can be.
Only Jesus gives us plenty
and fills us with His peace.

Jesus loves you, dear girl and boy;
each good gift comes from above.
He comes to give you hope and joy
and fill your hungry lives with love.

Dear Parent,

Everywhere Jesus went, people followed. They wanted to hear Him preach and to see His miracles. The people didn't quite understand yet, who Jesus was. (Even the apostles weren't fully understanding of Jesus' divinity.) Yet they flocked to Him because they couldn't get enough.

The people were hungry. Literally and figuratively, they needed nourishment, and when Jesus "saw the crowds, He had compassion for them, because they were …like sheep without a shepherd" (Matthew 9:36). The Good Shepherd provided physical food for the crowd and fed them with spiritual food as well.

Of all Jesus' miracles that are recorded in the Bible, the feeding of the five thousand is the only one mentioned in all four gospels. This miracle shows that Jesus has authority over nature. It proves His deity. It also gives an example of the office of ministry. Just as Jesus gave the apostles responsibility to distribute the food to the people, pastors today distribute the Lord's Supper. Like the crowd that day, who ate until they were satisfied, we go to the Lord's Supper and are fed with bread that gives eternal life.

The Editor